Winner's Information

Name ....

Email ....

Phone ....

Copyright © 2023 by Sandra Onye

All rights reserved. No part of this publication may be reproduced or used in any manner without the prior written permission of the copyright owner.

ISBN: 979-8-218-20155-5
Edited by Global Bookshelves International, LLC
Cover art and layout by Theary Chhim, PharmD

About the *Winning Is in My DNA: 15 Minutes of Daily Self-Reflection Journal*

Knowing where to begin when journaling can be confusing at times. The *Winning Is in My DNA: 15 Minutes of Daily Self-Reflection Journal* offers guidance on journaling effectively and purposefully. This journal provides a unique way of journaling that pushes you to reflect on your wins, allows you to acknowledge your feelings about the successes, and identifies areas to improve or conquer. It also offers a place for self-awareness and self-reflection on who you have been, who you are, and who you want to become—a winner.

I have been journaling since I was a teenager. Looking back at my old journal, I realized I'd been writing without purpose. I also journaled during my most difficult moments. It was helpful because it was a place to vent, but it rarely highlighted the good times, all my accomplishments, or my wins.

The idea for a "win journal" came at a time when it seemed like I was doing a lot but could not account for anything at the end of the day. I would go home exhausted and down, spend all my energy focusing on what I hadn't accomplished, and stress my failures and weaknesses. I would write down all these inadequacies as I have always done. I began to ask myself, "You can't be all that bad; there must be some things you are good at, right?" As I kept reflecting on my day-to-day activities, I realized I had won but never took the time to address them. I decided to start jotting my wins, no matter how little these wins may seem, and dedicate time to reflect on my accomplishments.

I began journaling my wins every day. Some days, I would have only three wins to list down; other days, when I put more effort, I would have up to ten wins jotted down. I noticed a boost in my self-confidence and a positive shift in my outlook on life. I also noticed that I actively looked for opportunities to win. My wins would range from opening the door for someone behind me to paying it forward at the local coffee shop. Recognizing these wins was terrific! Since then, I've been taking the time to reflect and jot down my wins daily. I also recorded how I felt about the day and things to improve on the next day or week. Journaling my successes helped me acknowledge that though life can be difficult, I can overcome life's obstacles. *Winning Is in My DNA: 15 Minutes of Daily Self-Reflection Journal* is my way of celebrating myself as a winner, and it can be the same for you.

You are responsible for tracking your daily triumphs, which then morph into weekly, monthly, and eventually yearly accomplishments. You must be proactive and intentional about choosing to focus on your greatness. Self-reflection and utilizing this journal are a great start to acknowledge and keep a record of your successes. This journal will guide you on how to document your life in a productive and empowering way.

Peter F. Drucker said, "The pertinent question is not how to do things right, but how to find the right things to do and concentrate resources and efforts on them."

Journaling your wins and successes is the right thing to do. So, let's get started.

YOU CAN DO THIS!

About the Author

Sandra Onye is the founder of WinDaily LLC, a mother, wife, Service Member, and a pharmacist by profession. She has over 25 years of experience journaling and has been dedicating daily self-reflection time since 2020. Sandra has deep-rooted passion for empowering others. Sandra is based in Georgia with her family, but travels the world with her career.

Examples of Using this Journal

 ## My Daily Wins
Write your wins, no matter how small!

1. I woke up before my alarm and made it to work on time.
2. I brought my lunch to work, and saved $10 that I would have spent otherwise.
3. I stood up for myself at school today, and noticed I was respected.
4. I went to the gym today!
5. I earned a promotion at work today.
6. I realized hard work does pay off.
7. I read to my kids today.
8. I began the journey of writing a book.
9. I began reading a book today.
10. I spent less time on social media.

 ## I Feel
Write how your wins make you feel.

1. I feel strong, powerful, and very proud of myself.
2. I feel like I am managing my money well.
3. I feel productive.

 ## Areas to Improve
Write these as "I will" statements.

1. I will finish responding to my emails by the end of the week.
2. I will pack my lunch at least three times a week.
3. I will get more rest by going to bed on time.

Quarterly Wins (Examples)

🎖️ My Top Three Wins for the Last Quarter
Write and reflect on the past quarter.

1. Getting promoted to Senior Manager at work.
2. Exercising three times a week, since I began going to the gym two months ago.
3. I began and finished reading a book.

My Wins Make Me Feel
Share how the wins from the last quarter make you feel.

1. I feel powerful and in control.
2. I feel like I can do anything I set my mind to do.
3. I feel blessed and highly favored.

Areas Needing More Time and Work
Write these as "I will" statements.

1. I will journal my wins more often.
2. I will surround myself with people who inspire me.
3. I will spend more time with my family.

LET'S GO!

What is your win today?

My Daily Wins
Write your wins, no matter how small!

Date ....

1. ....
2. ....
3. ....
4. ....
5. ....
6. ....
7. ....
8. ....
9. ....
10. ....

I Feel
Write how your wins make you feel.

1. ....
2. ....
3. ....

Areas to Improve
Write these as "I will" statements.

1. ....
2. ....
3. ....

Notes:

My Daily Wins
Write your wins, no matter how small!

Date ....

1. ....
2. ....
3. ....
4. ....
5. ....
6. ....
7. ....
8. ....
9. ....
10. ....

I Feel
Write how your wins make you feel.

1. ....
2. ....
3. ....

Areas to Improve
Write these as "I will" statements.

1. ....
2. ....
3. ....

Notes:

My Daily Wins
Write your wins, no matter how small!

Date ....

1. ....
2. ....
3. ....
4. ....
5. ....
6. ....
7. ....
8. ....
9. ....
10. ....

I Feel
Write how your wins make you feel.

1. ....
2. ....
3. ....

Areas to Improve
Write these as "I will" statements.

1. ....
2. ....
3. ....

Notes:

My Daily Wins
Write your wins, no matter how small!

Date ....

1. ....
2. ....
3. ....
4. ....
5. ....
6. ....
7. ....
8. ....
9. ....
10. ....

I Feel
Write how your wins make you feel.

1. ....
2. ....
3. ....

Areas to Improve
Write these as "I will" statements.

1. ....
2. ....
3. ....

Notes:

My Daily Wins

Date ....

Write your wins, no matter how small!

1. ....
2. ....
3. ....
4. ....
5. ....
6. ....
7. ....
8. ....
9. ....
10. ....

I Feel

Write how your wins make you feel.

1. ....
2. ....
3. ....

Areas to Improve

Write these as "I will" statements.

1. ....
2. ....
3. ....

Notes:

My Daily Wins
Write your wins, no matter how small!

Date ....

1. ....
2. ....
3. ....
4. ....
5. ....
6. ....
7. ....
8. ....
9. ....
10. ....

I Feel
Write how your wins make you feel.

1. ....
2. ....
3. ....

Areas to Improve
Write these as "I will" statements.

1. ....
2. ....
3. ....

Notes:

My Daily Wins
Write your wins, no matter how small!

Date ....

1. ....
2. ....
3. ....
4. ....
5. ....
6. ....
7. ....
8. ....
9. ....
10. ....

I Feel
Write how your wins make you feel.

1. ....
2. ....
3. ....

Areas to Improve
Write these as "I will" statements.

1. ....
2. ....
3. ....

Notes:

My Daily Wins
Write your wins, no matter how small!

Date ....

1. ....
2. ....
3. ....
4. ....
5. ....
6. ....
7. ....
8. ....
9. ....
10. ....

I Feel
Write how your wins make you feel.

1. ....
2. ....
3. ....

Areas to Improve
Write these as "I will" statements.

1. ....
2. ....
3. ....

Notes:

My Daily Wins
Write your wins, no matter how small!

Date ....

1. ....
2. ....
3. ....
4. ....
5. ....
6. ....
7. ....
8. ....
9. ....
10. ....

I Feel
Write how your wins make you feel.

1. ....
2. ....
3. ....

Areas to Improve
Write these as "I will" statements.

1. ....
2. ....
3. ....

Notes:

My Daily Wins
Write your wins, no matter how small!

Date ....

1. ....
2. ....
3. ....
4. ....
5. ....
6. ....
7. ....
8. ....
9. ....
10. ....

I Feel
Write how your wins make you feel.

1. ....
2. ....
3. ....

Areas to Improve
Write these as "I will" statements.

1. ....
2. ....
3. ....

Notes:

My Daily Wins
Write your wins, no matter how small!

Date ....

1. ....
2. ....
3. ....
4. ....
5. ....
6. ....
7. ....
8. ....
9. ....
10. ....

I Feel
Write how your wins make you feel.

1. ....
2. ....
3. ....

Areas to Improve
Write these as "I will" statements.

1. ....
2. ....
3. ....

Notes:

My Daily Wins
Write your wins, no matter how small!

Date ....

1. ....
2. ....
3. ....
4. ....
5. ....
6. ....
7. ....
8. ....
9. ....
10. ....

I Feel
Write how your wins make you feel.

1. ....
2. ....
3. ....

Areas to Improve
Write these as "I will" statements.

1. ....
2. ....
3. ....

Notes:

My Daily Wins
Write your wins, no matter how small!

Date ....

1. ....
2. ....
3. ....
4. ....
5. ....
6. ....
7. ....
8. ....
9. ....
10. ....

I Feel
Write how your wins make you feel.

1. ....
2. ....
3. ....

Areas to Improve
Write these as "I will" statements.

1. ....
2. ....
3. ....

Notes:

My Daily Wins
Write your wins, no matter how small!

Date ....

1. ....
2. ....
3. ....
4. ....
5. ....
6. ....
7. ....
8. ....
9. ....
10. ....

I Feel
Write how your wins make you feel.

1. ....
2. ....
3. ....

Areas to Improve
Write these as "I will" statements.

1. ....
2. ....
3. ....

Notes:

My Daily Wins
Write your wins, no matter how small!

Date ....

1. ....
2. ....
3. ....
4. ....
5. ....
6. ....
7. ....
8. ....
9. ....
10. ....

I Feel
Write how your wins make you feel.

1. ....
2. ....
3. ....

Areas to Improve
Write these as "I will" statements.

1. ....
2. ....
3. ....

Notes:

My Daily Wins
Write your wins, no matter how small!

Date ....

1. ....
2. ....
3. ....
4. ....
5. ....
6. ....
7. ....
8. ....
9. ....
10. ....

I Feel
Write how your wins make you feel.

1. ....
2. ....
3. ....

Areas to Improve
Write these as "I will" statements.

1. ....
2. ....
3. ....

Notes:

My Daily Wins
Write your wins, no matter how small!

Date ....

1. ....
2. ....
3. ....
4. ....
5. ....
6. ....
7. ....
8. ....
9. ....
10. ....

I Feel
Write how your wins make you feel.

1. ....
2. ....
3. ....

Areas to Improve
Write these as "I will" statements.

1. ....
2. ....
3. ....

Notes:

My Daily Wins
Write your wins, no matter how small!

Date ....

1. ....
2. ....
3. ....
4. ....
5. ....
6. ....
7. ....
8. ....
9. ....
10. ....

I Feel
Write how your wins make you feel.

1. ....
2. ....
3. ....

Areas to Improve
Write these as "I will" statements.

1. ....
2. ....
3. ....

Notes:

My Daily Wins
Write your wins, no matter how small!

Date ....

1. ....
2. ....
3. ....
4. ....
5. ....
6. ....
7. ....
8. ....
9. ....
10. ....

I Feel
Write how your wins make you feel.

1. ....
2. ....
3. ....

Areas to Improve
Write these as "I will" statements.

1. ....
2. ....
3. ....

Notes:

My Daily Wins
Write your wins, no matter how small!

Date ....

1. ....
2. ....
3. ....
4. ....
5. ....
6. ....
7. ....
8. ....
9. ....
10. ....

I Feel
Write how your wins make you feel.

1. ....
2. ....
3. ....

Areas to Improve
Write these as "I will" statements.

1. ....
2. ....
3. ....

Notes:

My Daily Wins
Write your wins, no matter how small!

Date ....

1. ....
2. ....
3. ....
4. ....
5. ....
6. ....
7. ....
8. ....
9. ....
10. ....

I Feel
Write how your wins make you feel.

1. ....
2. ....
3. ....

Areas to Improve
Write these as "I will" statements.

1. ....
2. ....
3. ....

Notes:

My Daily Wins
Write your wins, no matter how small!

Date ....

1. ....
2. ....
3. ....
4. ....
5. ....
6. ....
7. ....
8. ....
9. ....
10. ....

I Feel
Write how your wins make you feel.

1. ....
2. ....
3. ....

Areas to Improve
Write these as "I will" statements.

1. ....
2. ....
3. ....

Notes:

My Daily Wins
Write your wins, no matter how small!

Date ....

1. ....
2. ....
3. ....
4. ....
5. ....
6. ....
7. ....
8. ....
9. ....
10. ....

I Feel
Write how your wins make you feel.

1. ....
2. ....
3. ....

Areas to Improve
Write these as "I will" statements.

1. ....
2. ....
3. ....

Notes:

My Daily Wins
Write your wins, no matter how small!

Date ....

1. ....
2. ....
3. ....
4. ....
5. ....
6. ....
7. ....
8. ....
9. ....
10. ....

I Feel
Write how your wins make you feel.

1. ....
2. ....
3. ....

Areas to Improve
Write these as "I will" statements.

1. ....
2. ....
3. ....

Notes:

My Daily Wins

Date ....

Write your wins, no matter how small!

1. ....
2. ....
3. ....
4. ....
5. ....
6. ....
7. ....
8. ....
9. ....
10. ....

I Feel

Write how your wins make you feel.

1. ....
2. ....
3. ....

Areas to Improve

Write these as "I will" statements.

1. ....
2. ....
3. ....

Notes:

My Daily Wins
Write your wins, no matter how small!

Date ....

1. ....
2. ....
3. ....
4. ....
5. ....
6. ....
7. ....
8. ....
9. ....
10. ....

I Feel
Write how your wins make you feel.

1. ....
2. ....
3. ....

Areas to Improve
Write these as "I will" statements.

1. ....
2. ....
3. ....

Notes:

My Daily Wins
Write your wins, no matter how small!

Date ....

1. ....
2. ....
3. ....
4. ....
5. ....
6. ....
7. ....
8. ....
9. ....
10. ....

I Feel
Write how your wins make you feel.

1. ....
2. ....
3. ....

Areas to Improve
Write these as "I will" statements.

1. ....
2. ....
3. ....

Notes:

My Daily Wins
Write your wins, no matter how small!

Date ....

1. ....
2. ....
3. ....
4. ....
5. ....
6. ....
7. ....
8. ....
9. ....
10. ....

I Feel
Write how your wins make you feel.

1. ....
2. ....
3. ....

Areas to Improve
Write these as "I will" statements.

1. ....
2. ....
3. ....

Notes:

My Daily Wins
Write your wins, no matter how small!

Date ....

1. ....
2. ....
3. ....
4. ....
5. ....
6. ....
7. ....
8. ....
9. ....
10. ....

I Feel
Write how your wins make you feel.

1. ....
2. ....
3. ....

Areas to Improve
Write these as "I will" statements.

1. ....
2. ....
3. ....

Notes:

My Daily Wins
Write your wins, no matter how small!

Date ....

1. ....
2. ....
3. ....
4. ....
5. ....
6. ....
7. ....
8. ....
9. ....
10. ....

I Feel
Write how your wins make you feel.

1. ....
2. ....
3. ....

Areas to Improve
Write these as "I will" statements.

1. ....
2. ....
3. ....

Notes:

My Daily Wins
Write your wins, no matter how small!

Date ....

1. ....
2. ....
3. ....
4. ....
5. ....
6. ....
7. ....
8. ....
9. ....
10. ....

I Feel
Write how your wins make you feel.

1. ....
2. ....
3. ....

Areas to Improve
Write these as "I will" statements.

1. ....
2. ....
3. ....

Notes:

My Daily Wins
Write your wins, no matter how small!

Date ....

1. ....
2. ....
3. ....
4. ....
5. ....
6. ....
7. ....
8. ....
9. ....
10. ....

I Feel
Write how your wins make you feel.

1. ....
2. ....
3. ....

Areas to Improve
Write these as "I will" statements.

1. ....
2. ....
3. ....

Notes:

My Daily Wins
Write your wins, no matter how small!

Date ....

1. ....
2. ....
3. ....
4. ....
5. ....
6. ....
7. ....
8. ....
9. ....
10. ....

I Feel
Write how your wins make you feel.

1. ....
2. ....
3. ....

Areas to Improve
Write these as "I will" statements.

1. ....
2. ....
3. ....

Notes:

My Daily Wins
Write your wins, no matter how small!

Date ....

1. ....
2. ....
3. ....
4. ....
5. ....
6. ....
7. ....
8. ....
9. ....
10. ....

I Feel
Write how your wins make you feel.

1. ....
2. ....
3. ....

Areas to Improve
Write these as "I will" statements.

1. ....
2. ....
3. ....

Notes:

My Daily Wins
Write your wins, no matter how small!

Date ....

1. ....
2. ....
3. ....
4. ....
5. ....
6. ....
7. ....
8. ....
9. ....
10. ....

I Feel
Write how your wins make you feel.

1. ....
2. ....
3. ....

Areas to Improve
Write these as "I will" statements.

1. ....
2. ....
3. ....

Notes:

My Daily Wins
Write your wins, no matter how small!

Date ....

1. ....
2. ....
3. ....
4. ....
5. ....
6. ....
7. ....
8. ....
9. ....
10. ....

I Feel
Write how your wins make you feel.

1. ....
2. ....
3. ....

Areas to Improve
Write these as "I will" statements.

1. ....
2. ....
3. ....

Notes:

My Daily Wins
Write your wins, no matter how small!

Date ....

1. ....
2. ....
3. ....
4. ....
5. ....
6. ....
7. ....
8. ....
9. ....
10. ....

I Feel
Write how your wins make you feel.

1. ....
2. ....
3. ....

Areas to Improve
Write these as "I will" statements.

1. ....
2. ....
3. ....

Notes:

My Daily Wins
Write your wins, no matter how small!

Date ....

1. ....
2. ....
3. ....
4. ....
5. ....
6. ....
7. ....
8. ....
9. ....
10. ....

I Feel
Write how your wins make you feel.

1. ....
2. ....
3. ....

Areas to Improve
Write these as "I will" statements.

1. ....
2. ....
3. ....

Notes:

My Daily Wins
Write your wins, no matter how small!

Date ....

1. ....
2. ....
3. ....
4. ....
5. ....
6. ....
7. ....
8. ....
9. ....
10. ....

I Feel
Write how your wins make you feel.

1. ....
2. ....
3. ....

Areas to Improve
Write these as "I will" statements.

1. ....
2. ....
3. ....

Notes:

My Daily Wins
Write your wins, no matter how small!

Date ....

1. ....
2. ....
3. ....
4. ....
5. ....
6. ....
7. ....
8. ....
9. ....
10. ....

I Feel
Write how your wins make you feel.

1. ....
2. ....
3. ....

Areas to Improve
Write these as "I will" statements.

1. ....
2. ....
3. ....

Notes:

My Daily Wins
Write your wins, no matter how small!

Date ....

1. ....
2. ....
3. ....
4. ....
5. ....
6. ....
7. ....
8. ....
9. ....
10. ....

I Feel
Write how your wins make you feel.

1. ....
2. ....
3. ....

Areas to Improve
Write these as "I will" statements.

1. ....
2. ....
3. ....

Notes:

My Daily Wins

Date ....

Write your wins, no matter how small!

1. ....
2. ....
3. ....
4. ....
5. ....
6. ....
7. ....
8. ....
9. ....
10. ....

I Feel

Write how your wins make you feel.

1. ....
2. ....
3. ....

Areas to Improve

Write these as "I will" statements.

1. ....
2. ....
3. ....

Notes:

My Daily Wins
Write your wins, no matter how small!

Date ....

1.
2.
3.
4.
5.
6.
7.
8.
9.
10.

I Feel
Write how your wins make you feel.

1.
2.
3.

Areas to Improve
Write these as "I will" statements.

1.
2.
3.

Notes:

My Daily Wins
Write your wins, no matter how small!

Date ....

1. ....
2. ....
3. ....
4. ....
5. ....
6. ....
7. ....
8. ....
9. ....
10. ....

I Feel
Write how your wins make you feel.

1. ....
2. ....
3. ....

Areas to Improve
Write these as "I will" statements.

1. ....
2. ....
3. ....

Notes:

My Daily Wins
Write your wins, no matter how small!

Date ....

1. ....
2. ....
3. ....
4. ....
5. ....
6. ....
7. ....
8. ....
9. ....
10. ....

I Feel
Write how your wins make you feel.

1. ....
2. ....
3. ....

Areas to Improve
Write these as "I will" statements.

1. ....
2. ....
3. ....

Notes:

My Daily Wins

Write your wins, no matter how small!

Date ....

1. ....
2. ....
3. ....
4. ....
5. ....
6. ....
7. ....
8. ....
9. ....
10. ....

I Feel

Write how your wins make you feel.

1. ....
2. ....
3. ....

Areas to Improve

Write these as "I will" statements.

1. ....
2. ....
3. ....

Notes:

My Daily Wins
Write your wins, no matter how small!

Date ....

1. ....
2. ....
3. ....
4. ....
5. ....
6. ....
7. ....
8. ....
9. ....
10. ....

I Feel
Write how your wins make you feel.

1. ....
2. ....
3. ....

Areas to Improve
Write these as "I will" statements.

1. ....
2. ....
3. ....

Notes:

My Daily Wins
Write your wins, no matter how small!

Date ....

1. ....
2. ....
3. ....
4. ....
5. ....
6. ....
7. ....
8. ....
9. ....
10. ....

I Feel
Write how your wins make you feel.

1. ....
2. ....
3. ....

Areas to Improve
Write these as "I will" statements.

1. ....
2. ....
3. ....

Notes:

My Daily Wins
Write your wins, no matter how small!

Date ....

1. ....
2. ....
3. ....
4. ....
5. ....
6. ....
7. ....
8. ....
9. ....
10. ....

I Feel
Write how your wins make you feel.

1. ....
2. ....
3. ....

Areas to Improve
Write these as "I will" statements.

1. ....
2. ....
3. ....

Notes:

My Daily Wins
Write your wins, no matter how small!

Date ....

1. ....
2. ....
3. ....
4. ....
5. ....
6. ....
7. ....
8. ....
9. ....
10. ....

I Feel
Write how your wins make you feel.

1. ....
2. ....
3. ....

Areas to Improve
Write these as "I will" statements.

1. ....
2. ....
3. ....

Notes:

My Daily Wins
Write your wins, no matter how small!

Date ....

1. ....
2. ....
3. ....
4. ....
5. ....
6. ....
7. ....
8. ....
9. ....
10. ....

I Feel
Write how your wins make you feel.

1. ....
2. ....
3. ....

Areas to Improve
Write these as "I will" statements.

1. ....
2. ....
3. ....

Notes:

My Daily Wins
Write your wins, no matter how small!

Date ....

1. ....
2. ....
3. ....
4. ....
5. ....
6. ....
7. ....
8. ....
9. ....
10. ....

I Feel
Write how your wins make you feel.

1. ....
2. ....
3. ....

Areas to Improve
Write these as "I will" statements.

1. ....
2. ....
3. ....

Notes:

My Daily Wins
Write your wins, no matter how small!

Date ....

1. ....
2. ....
3. ....
4. ....
5. ....
6. ....
7. ....
8. ....
9. ....
10. ....

I Feel
Write how your wins make you feel.

1. ....
2. ....
3. ....

Areas to Improve
Write these as "I will" statements.

1. ....
2. ....
3. ....

Notes:

My Daily Wins
Write your wins, no matter how small!

Date ....

1. ....
2. ....
3. ....
4. ....
5. ....
6. ....
7. ....
8. ....
9. ....
10. ....

I Feel
Write how your wins make you feel.

1. ....
2. ....
3. ....

Areas to Improve
Write these as "I will" statements.

1. ....
2. ....
3. ....

Notes:

My Daily Wins
Write your wins, no matter how small!

Date ....

1. ....
2. ....
3. ....
4. ....
5. ....
6. ....
7. ....
8. ....
9. ....
10. ....

I Feel
Write how your wins make you feel.

1. ....
2. ....
3. ....

Areas to Improve
Write these as "I will" statements.

1. ....
2. ....
3. ....

Notes:

My Daily Wins
Write your wins, no matter how small!

Date ....

1. ....
2. ....
3. ....
4. ....
5. ....
6. ....
7. ....
8. ....
9. ....
10. ....

I Feel
Write how your wins make you feel.

1. ....
2. ....
3. ....

Areas to Improve
Write these as "I will" statements.

1. ....
2. ....
3. ....

Notes:

My Daily Wins
Write your wins, no matter how small!

Date ....

1. ....
2. ....
3. ....
4. ....
5. ....
6. ....
7. ....
8. ....
9. ....
10. ....

I Feel
Write how your wins make you feel.

1. ....
2. ....
3. ....

Areas to Improve
Write these as "I will" statements.

1. ....
2. ....
3. ....

Notes:

My Daily Wins
Write your wins, no matter how small!

Date ....

1. ....
2. ....
3. ....
4. ....
5. ....
6. ....
7. ....
8. ....
9. ....
10. ....

I Feel
Write how your wins make you feel.

1. ....
2. ....
3. ....

Areas to Improve
Write these as "I will" statements.

1. ....
2. ....
3. ....

Notes:

My Daily Wins
Write your wins, no matter how small!

Date ....

1. ....
2. ....
3. ....
4. ....
5. ....
6. ....
7. ....
8. ....
9. ....
10. ....

I Feel
Write how your wins make you feel.

1. ....
2. ....
3. ....

Areas to Improve
Write these as "I will" statements.

1. ....
2. ....
3. ....

Notes:

My Daily Wins

Write your wins, no matter how small!

Date ....

1. ....
2. ....
3. ....
4. ....
5. ....
6. ....
7. ....
8. ....
9. ....
10. ....

I Feel

Write how your wins make you feel.

1. ....
2. ....
3. ....

Areas to Improve

Write these as "I will" statements.

1. ....
2. ....
3. ....

Notes:

My Daily Wins
Write your wins, no matter how small!

Date ....

1. ....
2. ....
3. ....
4. ....
5. ....
6. ....
7. ....
8. ....
9. ....
10. ....

I Feel
Write how your wins make you feel.

1. ....
2. ....
3. ....

Areas to Improve
Write these as "I will" statements.

1. ....
2. ....
3. ....

Notes:

My Daily Wins
Write your wins, no matter how small!

Date ....

1. ....
2. ....
3. ....
4. ....
5. ....
6. ....
7. ....
8. ....
9. ....
10. ....

I Feel
Write how your wins make you feel.

1. ....
2. ....
3. ....

Areas to Improve
Write these as "I will" statements.

1. ....
2. ....
3. ....

Notes:

My Daily Wins
Write your wins, no matter how small!

Date ....

1. ....
2. ....
3. ....
4. ....
5. ....
6. ....
7. ....
8. ....
9. ....
10. ....

I Feel
Write how your wins make you feel.

1. ....
2. ....
3. ....

Areas to Improve
Write these as "I will" statements.

1. ....
2. ....
3. ....

Notes:

My Daily Wins

Write your wins, no matter how small!

Date ....

1. ....
2. ....
3. ....
4. ....
5. ....
6. ....
7. ....
8. ....
9. ....
10. ....

I Feel

Write how your wins make you feel.

1. ....
2. ....
3. ....

Areas to Improve

Write these as "I will" statements.

1. ....
2. ....
3. ....

Notes:

My Daily Wins
Write your wins, no matter how small!

Date ....

1. ....
2. ....
3. ....
4. ....
5. ....
6. ....
7. ....
8. ....
9. ....
10. ....

I Feel
Write how your wins make you feel.

1. ....
2. ....
3. ....

Areas to Improve
Write these as "I will" statements.

1. ....
2. ....
3. ....

Notes:

My Daily Wins
Write your wins, no matter how small!

Date ....

1. ....
2. ....
3. ....
4. ....
5. ....
6. ....
7. ....
8. ....
9. ....
10. ....

I Feel
Write how your wins make you feel.

1. ....
2. ....
3. ....

Areas to Improve
Write these as "I will" statements.

1. ....
2. ....
3. ....

Notes:

My Daily Wins
Write your wins, no matter how small!

Date ....

1. ....
2. ....
3. ....
4. ....
5. ....
6. ....
7. ....
8. ....
9. ....
10. ....

I Feel
Write how your wins make you feel.

1. ....
2. ....
3. ....

Areas to Improve
Write these as "I will" statements.

1. ....
2. ....
3. ....

Notes:

My Daily Wins

Date ....

Write your wins, no matter how small!

1. ....
2. ....
3. ....
4. ....
5. ....
6. ....
7. ....
8. ....
9. ....
10. ....

I Feel

Write how your wins make you feel.

1. ....
2. ....
3. ....

Areas to Improve

Write these as "I will" statements.

1. ....
2. ....
3. ....

Notes:

My Daily Wins
Write your wins, no matter how small!

Date ....

1. ....
2. ....
3. ....
4. ....
5. ....
6. ....
7. ....
8. ....
9. ....
10. ....

I Feel
Write how your wins make you feel.

1. ....
2. ....
3. ....

Areas to Improve
Write these as "I will" statements.

1. ....
2. ....
3. ....

Notes:

My Daily Wins
Write your wins, no matter how small!

Date ....

1. ....
2. ....
3. ....
4. ....
5. ....
6. ....
7. ....
8. ....
9. ....
10. ....

I Feel
Write how your wins make you feel.

1. ....
2. ....
3. ....

Areas to Improve
Write these as "I will" statements.

1. ....
2. ....
3. ....

Notes:

My Daily Wins
Write your wins, no matter how small!

Date ....

1. ....
2. ....
3. ....
4. ....
5. ....
6. ....
7. ....
8. ....
9. ....
10. ....

I Feel
Write how your wins make you feel.

1. ....
2. ....
3. ....

Areas to Improve
Write these as "I will" statements.

1. ....
2. ....
3. ....

Notes:

My Daily Wins
Write your wins, no matter how small!

Date ....

1. ...
2. ...
3. ...
4. ...
5. ...
6. ...
7. ...
8. ...
9. ...
10. ...

I Feel
Write how your wins make you feel.

1. ...
2. ...
3. ...

Areas to Improve
Write these as "I will" statements.

1. ...
2. ...
3. ...

Notes:

My Daily Wins
Write your wins, no matter how small!

Date ....

1. ....
2. ....
3. ....
4. ....
5. ....
6. ....
7. ....
8. ....
9. ....
10. ....

I Feel
Write how your wins make you feel.

1. ....
2. ....
3. ....

Areas to Improve
Write these as "I will" statements.

1. ....
2. ....
3. ....

Notes:

My Daily Wins
Write your wins, no matter how small!

Date ....

1. ....
2. ....
3. ....
4. ....
5. ....
6. ....
7. ....
8. ....
9. ....
10. ....

I Feel
Write how your wins make you feel.

1. ....
2. ....
3. ....

Areas to Improve
Write these as "I will" statements.

1. ....
2. ....
3. ....

Notes:

My Daily Wins
Write your wins, no matter how small!

Date ....

1. ....
2. ....
3. ....
4. ....
5. ....
6. ....
7. ....
8. ....
9. ....
10. ....

I Feel
Write how your wins make you feel.

1. ....
2. ....
3. ....

Areas to Improve
Write these as "I will" statements.

1. ....
2. ....
3. ....

Notes:

My Daily Wins
Write your wins, no matter how small!

Date ....

1. ....
2. ....
3. ....
4. ....
5. ....
6. ....
7. ....
8. ....
9. ....
10. ....

I Feel
Write how your wins make you feel.

1. ....
2. ....
3. ....

Areas to Improve
Write these as "I will" statements.

1. ....
2. ....
3. ....

Notes:

My Daily Wins
Write your wins, no matter how small!

Date ....

1. ....
2. ....
3. ....
4. ....
5. ....
6. ....
7. ....
8. ....
9. ....
10. ....

I Feel
Write how your wins make you feel.

1. ....
2. ....
3. ....

Areas to Improve
Write these as "I will" statements.

1. ....
2. ....
3. ....

Notes:

My Daily Wins
Write your wins, no matter how small!

Date ....

1. ....
2. ....
3. ....
4. ....
5. ....
6. ....
7. ....
8. ....
9. ....
10. ....

I Feel
Write how your wins make you feel.

1. ....
2. ....
3. ....

Areas to Improve
Write these as "I will" statements.

1. ....
2. ....
3. ....

Notes:

My Daily Wins
Write your wins, no matter how small!

Date ....

1. ....
2. ....
3. ....
4. ....
5. ....
6. ....
7. ....
8. ....
9. ....
10. ....

I Feel
Write how your wins make you feel.

1. ....
2. ....
3. ....

Areas to Improve
Write these as "I will" statements.

1. ....
2. ....
3. ....

Notes:

My Daily Wins
Write your wins, no matter how small!

Date ....

1. ....
2. ....
3. ....
4. ....
5. ....
6. ....
7. ....
8. ....
9. ....
10. ....

I Feel
Write how your wins make you feel.

1. ....
2. ....
3. ....

Areas to Improve
Write these as "I will" statements.

1. ....
2. ....
3. ....

Notes:

My Daily Wins
Write your wins, no matter how small!

Date ....

1. ....
2. ....
3. ....
4. ....
5. ....
6. ....
7. ....
8. ....
9. ....
10. ....

I Feel
Write how your wins make you feel.

1. ....
2. ....
3. ....

Areas to Improve
Write these as "I will" statements.

1. ....
2. ....
3. ....

Notes:

My Daily Wins
Write your wins, no matter how small!

Date ....

1. ....
2. ....
3. ....
4. ....
5. ....
6. ....
7. ....
8. ....
9. ....
10. ....

I Feel
Write how your wins make you feel.

1. ....
2. ....
3. ....

Areas to Improve
Write these as "I will" statements.

1. ....
2. ....
3. ....

Notes:

My Daily Wins
Write your wins, no matter how small!

Date ....

1. ....
2. ....
3. ....
4. ....
5. ....
6. ....
7. ....
8. ....
9. ....
10. ....

I Feel
Write how your wins make you feel.

1. ....
2. ....
3. ....

Areas to Improve
Write these as "I will" statements.

1. ....
2. ....
3. ....

Notes:

My Daily Wins
Write your wins, no matter how small!

Date ....

1. ....
2. ....
3. ....
4. ....
5. ....
6. ....
7. ....
8. ....
9. ....
10. ....

I Feel
Write how your wins make you feel.

1. ....
2. ....
3. ....

Areas to Improve
Write these as "I will" statements.

1. ....
2. ....
3. ....

Notes:

My Daily Wins
Write your wins, no matter how small!

Date ....

1. ....
2. ....
3. ....
4. ....
5. ....
6. ....
7. ....
8. ....
9. ....
10. ....

I Feel
Write how your wins make you feel.

1. ....
2. ....
3. ....

Areas to Improve
Write these as "I will" statements.

1. ....
2. ....
3. ....

Notes:

My Daily Wins
Write your wins, no matter how small!

Date ....

1. ....
2. ....
3. ....
4. ....
5. ....
6. ....
7. ....
8. ....
9. ....
10. ....

I Feel
Write how your wins make you feel.

1. ....
2. ....
3. ....

Areas to Improve
Write these as "I will" statements.

1. ....
2. ....
3. ....

Notes:

My Daily Wins
Write your wins, no matter how small!

Date ....

1. ....
2. ....
3. ....
4. ....
5. ....
6. ....
7. ....
8. ....
9. ....
10. ....

I Feel
Write how your wins make you feel.

1. ....
2. ....
3. ....

Areas to Improve
Write these as "I will" statements.

1. ....
2. ....
3. ....

Notes:

My Daily Wins
Write your wins, no matter how small!

Date ....

1. ....
2. ....
3. ....
4. ....
5. ....
6. ....
7. ....
8. ....
9. ....
10. ....

I Feel
Write how your wins make you feel.

1. ....
2. ....
3. ....

Areas to Improve
Write these as "I will" statements.

1. ....
2. ....
3. ....

Notes:

My Daily Wins
Write your wins, no matter how small!

Date ....

1. ....
2. ....
3. ....
4. ....
5. ....
6. ....
7. ....
8. ....
9. ....
10. ....

I Feel
Write how your wins make you feel.

1. ....
2. ....
3. ....

Areas to Improve
Write these as "I will" statements.

1. ....
2. ....
3. ....

Notes:

My Daily Wins
Write your wins, no matter how small!

Date ....

1. ....
2. ....
3. ....
4. ....
5. ....
6. ....
7. ....
8. ....
9. ....
10. ....

I Feel
Write how your wins make you feel.

1. ....
2. ....
3. ....

Areas to Improve
Write these as "I will" statements.

1. ....
2. ....
3. ....

Notes:

Quarterly Wins

My Top Three Wins for the Last Quarter   Date ....
Write and reflect on the past quarter.

1. ....
2. ....
3. ....

My Wins Make Me Feel
Share how the wins from the last quarter make you feel.

1. ....
2. ....
3. ....

Areas Needing More Time and Work
Write these as "I will" statements.

1. ....
2. ....
3. ....

Notes:

My Daily Wins
Write your wins, no matter how small!

Date ....

1. ....
2. ....
3. ....
4. ....
5. ....
6. ....
7. ....
8. ....
9. ....
10. ....

I Feel
Write how your wins make you feel.

1. ....
2. ....
3. ....

Areas to Improve
Write these as "I will" statements.

1. ....
2. ....
3. ....

Notes:

My Daily Wins
Write your wins, no matter how small!

Date ....

1. ....
2. ....
3. ....
4. ....
5. ....
6. ....
7. ....
8. ....
9. ....
10. ....

I Feel
Write how your wins make you feel.

1. ....
2. ....
3. ....

Areas to Improve
Write these as "I will" statements.

1. ....
2. ....
3. ....

Notes:

My Daily Wins
Write your wins, no matter how small!

Date ....

1. ....
2. ....
3. ....
4. ....
5. ....
6. ....
7. ....
8. ....
9. ....
10. ....

I Feel
Write how your wins make you feel.

1. ....
2. ....
3. ....

Areas to Improve
Write these as "I will" statements.

1. ....
2. ....
3. ....

Notes:

My Daily Wins
Write your wins, no matter how small!

Date ....

1. ....
2. ....
3. ....
4. ....
5. ....
6. ....
7. ....
8. ....
9. ....
10. ....

I Feel
Write how your wins make you feel.

1. ....
2. ....
3. ....

Areas to Improve
Write these as "I will" statements.

1. ....
2. ....
3. ....

Notes:

My Daily Wins
Write your wins, no matter how small!

Date ....

1. ....
2. ....
3. ....
4. ....
5. ....
6. ....
7. ....
8. ....
9. ....
10. ....

I Feel
Write how your wins make you feel.

1. ....
2. ....
3. ....

Areas to Improve
Write these as "I will" statements.

1. ....
2. ....
3. ....

Notes:

My Daily Wins
Write your wins, no matter how small!

Date ....

1. ....
2. ....
3. ....
4. ....
5. ....
6. ....
7. ....
8. ....
9. ....
10. ....

I Feel
Write how your wins make you feel.

1. ....
2. ....
3. ....

Areas to Improve
Write these as "I will" statements.

1. ....
2. ....
3. ....

Notes:

My Daily Wins
Write your wins, no matter how small!

Date ....

1. ....
2. ....
3. ....
4. ....
5. ....
6. ....
7. ....
8. ....
9. ....
10. ....

I Feel
Write how your wins make you feel.

1. ....
2. ....
3. ....

Areas to Improve
Write these as "I will" statements.

1. ....
2. ....
3. ....

Notes:

My Daily Wins
Write your wins, no matter how small!

Date ....

1. ....
2. ....
3. ....
4. ....
5. ....
6. ....
7. ....
8. ....
9. ....
10. ....

I Feel
Write how your wins make you feel.

1. ....
2. ....
3. ....

Areas to Improve
Write these as "I will" statements.

1. ....
2. ....
3. ....

Notes:

My Daily Wins
Write your wins, no matter how small!

Date ....

1. ....
2. ....
3. ....
4. ....
5. ....
6. ....
7. ....
8. ....
9. ....
10. ....

I Feel
Write how your wins make you feel.

1. ....
2. ....
3. ....

Areas to Improve
Write these as "I will" statements.

1. ....
2. ....
3. ....

Notes:

My Daily Wins
Write your wins, no matter how small!

Date ....

1. ....
2. ....
3. ....
4. ....
5. ....
6. ....
7. ....
8. ....
9. ....
10. ....

I Feel
Write how your wins make you feel.

1. ....
2. ....
3. ....

Areas to Improve
Write these as "I will" statements.

1. ....
2. ....
3. ....

Notes:

My Daily Wins
Write your wins, no matter how small!

Date ....

1. ....
2. ....
3. ....
4. ....
5. ....
6. ....
7. ....
8. ....
9. ....
10. ....

I Feel
Write how your wins make you feel.

1. ....
2. ....
3. ....

Areas to Improve
Write these as "I will" statements.

1. ....
2. ....
3. ....

Notes:

My Daily Wins
Write your wins, no matter how small!

Date ....

1. ....
2. ....
3. ....
4. ....
5. ....
6. ....
7. ....
8. ....
9. ....
10. ....

I Feel
Write how your wins make you feel.

1. ....
2. ....
3. ....

Areas to Improve
Write these as "I will" statements.

1. ....
2. ....
3. ....

Notes:

My Daily Wins
Write your wins, no matter how small!

Date ....

1. ....
2. ....
3. ....
4. ....
5. ....
6. ....
7. ....
8. ....
9. ....
10. ....

I Feel
Write how your wins make you feel.

1. ....
2. ....
3. ....

Areas to Improve
Write these as "I will" statements.

1. ....
2. ....
3. ....

Notes:

My Daily Wins
Write your wins, no matter how small!

Date ....

1. ....
2. ....
3. ....
4. ....
5. ....
6. ....
7. ....
8. ....
9. ....
10. ....

I Feel
Write how your wins make you feel.

1. ....
2. ....
3. ....

Areas to Improve
Write these as "I will" statements.

1. ....
2. ....
3. ....

Notes:

My Daily Wins
Write your wins, no matter how small!

Date ....

1. ....
2. ....
3. ....
4. ....
5. ....
6. ....
7. ....
8. ....
9. ....
10. ....

I Feel
Write how your wins make you feel.

1. ....
2. ....
3. ....

Areas to Improve
Write these as "I will" statements.

1. ....
2. ....
3. ....

Notes:

My Daily Wins
Write your wins, no matter how small!

Date ....

1. ....
2. ....
3. ....
4. ....
5. ....
6. ....
7. ....
8. ....
9. ....
10. ....

I Feel
Write how your wins make you feel.

1. ....
2. ....
3. ....

Areas to Improve
Write these as "I will" statements.

1. ....
2. ....
3. ....

Notes:

My Daily Wins

Write your wins, no matter how small!

Date ....

1. ....
2. ....
3. ....
4. ....
5. ....
6. ....
7. ....
8. ....
9. ....
10. ....

I Feel

Write how your wins make you feel.

1. ....
2. ....
3. ....

Areas to Improve

Write these as "I will" statements.

1. ....
2. ....
3. ....

Notes:

My Daily Wins
Write your wins, no matter how small!

Date ....

1. ....
2. ....
3. ....
4. ....
5. ....
6. ....
7. ....
8. ....
9. ....
10. ....

I Feel
Write how your wins make you feel.

1. ....
2. ....
3. ....

Areas to Improve
Write these as "I will" statements.

1. ....
2. ....
3. ....

Notes:

My Daily Wins
Write your wins, no matter how small!

Date ....

1. ....
2. ....
3. ....
4. ....
5. ....
6. ....
7. ....
8. ....
9. ....
10. ....

I Feel
Write how your wins make you feel.

1. ....
2. ....
3. ....

Areas to Improve
Write these as "I will" statements.

1. ....
2. ....
3. ....

Notes:

My Daily Wins
Write your wins, no matter how small!

Date ....

1. ....
2. ....
3. ....
4. ....
5. ....
6. ....
7. ....
8. ....
9. ....
10. ....

I Feel
Write how your wins make you feel.

1. ....
2. ....
3. ....

Areas to Improve
Write these as "I will" statements.

1. ....
2. ....
3. ....

Notes:

My Daily Wins
Write your wins, no matter how small!

Date ....

1. ....
2. ....
3. ....
4. ....
5. ....
6. ....
7. ....
8. ....
9. ....
10. ....

I Feel
Write how your wins make you feel.

1. ....
2. ....
3. ....

Areas to Improve
Write these as "I will" statements.

1. ....
2. ....
3. ....

Notes:

My Daily Wins
Write your wins, no matter how small!

Date ....

1. ....
2. ....
3. ....
4. ....
5. ....
6. ....
7. ....
8. ....
9. ....
10. ....

I Feel
Write how your wins make you feel.

1. ....
2. ....
3. ....

Areas to Improve
Write these as "I will" statements.

1. ....
2. ....
3. ....

Notes:

My Daily Wins
Write your wins, no matter how small!

Date ....

1. ....
2. ....
3. ....
4. ....
5. ....
6. ....
7. ....
8. ....
9. ....
10. ....

I Feel
Write how your wins make you feel.

1. ....
2. ....
3. ....

Areas to Improve
Write these as "I will" statements.

1. ....
2. ....
3. ....

Notes:

My Daily Wins
Write your wins, no matter how small!

Date ....

1. ....
2. ....
3. ....
4. ....
5. ....
6. ....
7. ....
8. ....
9. ....
10. ....

I Feel
Write how your wins make you feel.

1. ....
2. ....
3. ....

Areas to Improve
Write these as "I will" statements.

1. ....
2. ....
3. ....

Notes:

My Daily Wins

Date ....

Write your wins, no matter how small!

1. ....
2. ....
3. ....
4. ....
5. ....
6. ....
7. ....
8. ....
9. ....
10. ....

I Feel
Write how your wins make you feel.

1. ....
2. ....
3. ....

Areas to Improve
Write these as "I will" statements.

1. ....
2. ....
3. ....

Notes:

My Daily Wins
Write your wins, no matter how small!

Date ....

1. ....
2. ....
3. ....
4. ....
5. ....
6. ....
7. ....
8. ....
9. ....
10. ....

I Feel
Write how your wins make you feel.

1. ....
2. ....
3. ....

Areas to Improve
Write these as "I will" statements.

1. ....
2. ....
3. ....

Notes:

My Daily Wins
Write your wins, no matter how small!

Date ....

1. ....
2. ....
3. ....
4. ....
5. ....
6. ....
7. ....
8. ....
9. ....
10. ....

I Feel
Write how your wins make you feel.

1. ....
2. ....
3. ....

Areas to Improve
Write these as "I will" statements.

1. ....
2. ....
3. ....

Notes:

My Daily Wins
Write your wins, no matter how small!

Date ....

1. ....
2. ....
3. ....
4. ....
5. ....
6. ....
7. ....
8. ....
9. ....
10. ....

I Feel
Write how your wins make you feel.

1. ....
2. ....
3. ....

Areas to Improve
Write these as "I will" statements.

1. ....
2. ....
3. ....

Notes:

My Daily Wins
Write your wins, no matter how small!

Date ....

1. ....
2. ....
3. ....
4. ....
5. ....
6. ....
7. ....
8. ....
9. ....
10. ....

I Feel
Write how your wins make you feel.

1. ....
2. ....
3. ....

Areas to Improve
Write these as "I will" statements.

1. ....
2. ....
3. ....

Notes:

My Daily Wins
Write your wins, no matter how small!

Date ....

1. ....
2. ....
3. ....
4. ....
5. ....
6. ....
7. ....
8. ....
9. ....
10. ....

I Feel
Write how your wins make you feel.

1. ....
2. ....
3. ....

Areas to Improve
Write these as "I will" statements.

1. ....
2. ....
3. ....

Notes:

My Daily Wins
Write your wins, no matter how small!

Date ....

1. ....
2. ....
3. ....
4. ....
5. ....
6. ....
7. ....
8. ....
9. ....
10. ....

I Feel
Write how your wins make you feel.

1. ....
2. ....
3. ....

Areas to Improve
Write these as "I will" statements.

1. ....
2. ....
3. ....

Notes:

My Daily Wins
Write your wins, no matter how small!

Date ....

1. ....
2. ....
3. ....
4. ....
5. ....
6. ....
7. ....
8. ....
9. ....
10. ....

I Feel
Write how your wins make you feel.

1. ....
2. ....
3. ....

Areas to Improve
Write these as "I will" statements.

1. ....
2. ....
3. ....

Notes:

My Daily Wins
Write your wins, no matter how small!

Date ....

1. ....
2. ....
3. ....
4. ....
5. ....
6. ....
7. ....
8. ....
9. ....
10. ....

I Feel
Write how your wins make you feel.

1. ....
2. ....
3. ....

Areas to Improve
Write these as "I will" statements.

1. ....
2. ....
3. ....

Notes:

My Daily Wins
Write your wins, no matter how small!

Date ....

1. ....
2. ....
3. ....
4. ....
5. ....
6. ....
7. ....
8. ....
9. ....
10. ....

I Feel
Write how your wins make you feel.

1. ....
2. ....
3. ....

Areas to Improve
Write these as "I will" statements.

1. ....
2. ....
3. ....

Notes:

My Daily Wins
Write your wins, no matter how small!

Date ....

1. ....
2. ....
3. ....
4. ....
5. ....
6. ....
7. ....
8. ....
9. ....
10. ....

I Feel
Write how your wins make you feel.

1. ....
2. ....
3. ....

Areas to Improve
Write these as "I will" statements.

1. ....
2. ....
3. ....

Notes:

My Daily Wins
Write your wins, no matter how small!

Date ....

1. ....
2. ....
3. ....
4. ....
5. ....
6. ....
7. ....
8. ....
9. ....
10. ....

I Feel
Write how your wins make you feel.

1. ....
2. ....
3. ....

Areas to Improve
Write these as "I will" statements.

1. ....
2. ....
3. ....

Notes:

My Daily Wins
Write your wins, no matter how small!

Date ....

1. ....
2. ....
3. ....
4. ....
5. ....
6. ....
7. ....
8. ....
9. ....
10. ....

I Feel
Write how your wins make you feel.

1. ....
2. ....
3. ....

Areas to Improve
Write these as "I will" statements.

1. ....
2. ....
3. ....

Notes:

My Daily Wins
Write your wins, no matter how small!

Date ....

1. ....
2. ....
3. ....
4. ....
5. ....
6. ....
7. ....
8. ....
9. ....
10. ....

I Feel
Write how your wins make you feel.

1. ....
2. ....
3. ....

Areas to Improve
Write these as "I will" statements.

1. ....
2. ....
3. ....

Notes:

My Daily Wins
Write your wins, no matter how small!

Date ....

1. ...
2. ...
3. ...
4. ...
5. ...
6. ...
7. ...
8. ...
9. ...
10. ...

I Feel
Write how your wins make you feel.

1. ...
2. ...
3. ...

Areas to Improve
Write these as "I will" statements.

1. ...
2. ...
3. ...

Notes:

My Daily Wins
Write your wins, no matter how small!

Date ....

1. ....
2. ....
3. ....
4. ....
5. ....
6. ....
7. ....
8. ....
9. ....
10. ....

I Feel
Write how your wins make you feel.

1. ....
2. ....
3. ....

Areas to Improve
Write these as "I will" statements.

1. ....
2. ....
3. ....

Notes:

My Daily Wins
Write your wins, no matter how small!

Date ....

1. ....
2. ....
3. ....
4. ....
5. ....
6. ....
7. ....
8. ....
9. ....
10. ....

I Feel
Write how your wins make you feel.

1. ....
2. ....
3. ....

Areas to Improve
Write these as "I will" statements.

1. ....
2. ....
3. ....

Notes:

My Daily Wins
Write your wins, no matter how small!

Date ....

1. ....
2. ....
3. ....
4. ....
5. ....
6. ....
7. ....
8. ....
9. ....
10. ....

I Feel
Write how your wins make you feel.

1. ....
2. ....
3. ....

Areas to Improve
Write these as "I will" statements.

1. ....
2. ....
3. ....

Notes:

My Daily Wins
Write your wins, no matter how small!

Date ....

1. ....
2. ....
3. ....
4. ....
5. ....
6. ....
7. ....
8. ....
9. ....
10. ....

I Feel
Write how your wins make you feel.

1. ....
2. ....
3. ....

Areas to Improve
Write these as "I will" statements.

1. ....
2. ....
3. ....

Notes:

My Daily Wins
Write your wins, no matter how small!

Date ....

1. ....
2. ....
3. ....
4. ....
5. ....
6. ....
7. ....
8. ....
9. ....
10. ....

I Feel
Write how your wins make you feel.

1. ....
2. ....
3. ....

Areas to Improve
Write these as "I will" statements.

1. ....
2. ....
3. ....

Notes:

My Daily Wins
Write your wins, no matter how small!

Date ....

1. ....
2. ....
3. ....
4. ....
5. ....
6. ....
7. ....
8. ....
9. ....
10. ....

I Feel
Write how your wins make you feel.

1. ....
2. ....
3. ....

Areas to Improve
Write these as "I will" statements.

1. ....
2. ....
3. ....

Notes:

My Daily Wins
Write your wins, no matter how small!

Date ....

1. ....
2. ....
3. ....
4. ....
5. ....
6. ....
7. ....
8. ....
9. ....
10. ....

I Feel
Write how your wins make you feel.

1. ....
2. ....
3. ....

Areas to Improve
Write these as "I will" statements.

1. ....
2. ....
3. ....

Notes:

My Daily Wins
Write your wins, no matter how small!

Date ....

1. ....
2. ....
3. ....
4. ....
5. ....
6. ....
7. ....
8. ....
9. ....
10. ....

I Feel
Write how your wins make you feel.

1. ....
2. ....
3. ....

Areas to Improve
Write these as "I will" statements.

1. ....
2. ....
3. ....

Notes:

My Daily Wins
Write your wins, no matter how small!

Date ....

1. ....
2. ....
3. ....
4. ....
5. ....
6. ....
7. ....
8. ....
9. ....
10. ....

I Feel
Write how your wins make you feel.

1. ....
2. ....
3. ....

Areas to Improve
Write these as "I will" statements.

1. ....
2. ....
3. ....

Notes:

My Daily Wins
Write your wins, no matter how small!

Date ....

1. ....
2. ....
3. ....
4. ....
5. ....
6. ....
7. ....
8. ....
9. ....
10. ....

I Feel
Write how your wins make you feel.

1. ....
2. ....
3. ....

Areas to Improve
Write these as "I will" statements.

1. ....
2. ....
3. ....

Notes:

My Daily Wins
Write your wins, no matter how small!

Date ....

1. ....
2. ....
3. ....
4. ....
5. ....
6. ....
7. ....
8. ....
9. ....
10. ....

I Feel
Write how your wins make you feel.

1. ....
2. ....
3. ....

Areas to Improve
Write these as "I will" statements.

1. ....
2. ....
3. ....

Notes:

My Daily Wins
Write your wins, no matter how small!

Date ....

1. ....
2. ....
3. ....
4. ....
5. ....
6. ....
7. ....
8. ....
9. ....
10. ....

I Feel
Write how your wins make you feel.

1. ....
2. ....
3. ....

Areas to Improve
Write these as "I will" statements.

1. ....
2. ....
3. ....

Notes:

My Daily Wins
Write your wins, no matter how small!

Date ....

1. ....
2. ....
3. ....
4. ....
5. ....
6. ....
7. ....
8. ....
9. ....
10. ....

I Feel
Write how your wins make you feel.

1. ....
2. ....
3. ....

Areas to Improve
Write these as "I will" statements.

1. ....
2. ....
3. ....

Notes:

My Daily Wins
Date ....

Write your wins, no matter how small!

1. ....
2. ....
3. ....
4. ....
5. ....
6. ....
7. ....
8. ....
9. ....
10. ....

I Feel
Write how your wins make you feel.

1. ....
2. ....
3. ....

Areas to Improve
Write these as "I will" statements.

1. ....
2. ....
3. ....

Notes:

My Daily Wins
Write your wins, no matter how small!

Date ....

1. ....
2. ....
3. ....
4. ....
5. ....
6. ....
7. ....
8. ....
9. ....
10. ....

I Feel
Write how your wins make you feel.

1. ....
2. ....
3. ....

Areas to Improve
Write these as "I will" statements.

1. ....
2. ....
3. ....

Notes:

My Daily Wins
Write your wins, no matter how small!

Date ....

1. ....
2. ....
3. ....
4. ....
5. ....
6. ....
7. ....
8. ....
9. ....
10. ....

I Feel
Write how your wins make you feel.

1. ....
2. ....
3. ....

Areas to Improve
Write these as "I will" statements.

1. ....
2. ....
3. ....

Notes:

My Daily Wins
Write your wins, no matter how small!

Date ....

1. ....
2. ....
3. ....
4. ....
5. ....
6. ....
7. ....
8. ....
9. ....
10. ....

I Feel
Write how your wins make you feel.

1. ....
2. ....
3. ....

Areas to Improve
Write these as "I will" statements.

1. ....
2. ....
3. ....

Notes:

My Daily Wins
Write your wins, no matter how small!

Date ....

1. ....
2. ....
3. ....
4. ....
5. ....
6. ....
7. ....
8. ....
9. ....
10. ....

I Feel
Write how your wins make you feel.

1. ....
2. ....
3. ....

Areas to Improve
Write these as "I will" statements.

1. ....
2. ....
3. ....

Notes:

My Daily Wins
Write your wins, no matter how small!

Date ....

1. ....
2. ....
3. ....
4. ....
5. ....
6. ....
7. ....
8. ....
9. ....
10. ....

I Feel
Write how your wins make you feel.

1. ....
2. ....
3. ....

Areas to Improve
Write these as "I will" statements.

1. ....
2. ....
3. ....

Notes:

My Daily Wins
Write your wins, no matter how small!

Date ....

1. ....
2. ....
3. ....
4. ....
5. ....
6. ....
7. ....
8. ....
9. ....
10. ....

I Feel
Write how your wins make you feel.

1. ....
2. ....
3. ....

Areas to Improve
Write these as "I will" statements.

1. ....
2. ....
3. ....

Notes:

My Daily Wins
Write your wins, no matter how small!

Date ....

1. ....
2. ....
3. ....
4. ....
5. ....
6. ....
7. ....
8. ....
9. ....
10. ....

I Feel
Write how your wins make you feel.

1. ....
2. ....
3. ....

Areas to Improve
Write these as "I will" statements.

1. ....
2. ....
3. ....

Notes:

My Daily Wins

Date ....

Write your wins, no matter how small!

1. ....
2. ....
3. ....
4. ....
5. ....
6. ....
7. ....
8. ....
9. ....
10. ....

I Feel

Write how your wins make you feel.

1. ....
2. ....
3. ....

Areas to Improve

Write these as "I will" statements.

1. ....
2. ....
3. ....

Notes:

My Daily Wins
Write your wins, no matter how small!

Date ....

1. ....
2. ....
3. ....
4. ....
5. ....
6. ....
7. ....
8. ....
9. ....
10. ....

I Feel
Write how your wins make you feel.

1. ....
2. ....
3. ....

Areas to Improve
Write these as "I will" statements.

1. ....
2. ....
3. ....

Notes:

My Daily Wins

Date ....

Write your wins, no matter how small!

1. ....
2. ....
3. ....
4. ....
5. ....
6. ....
7. ....
8. ....
9. ....
10. ....

I Feel

Write how your wins make you feel.

1. ....
2. ....
3. ....

Areas to Improve

Write these as "I will" statements.

1. ....
2. ....
3. ....

Notes:

My Daily Wins
Write your wins, no matter how small!

Date ....

1. ....
2. ....
3. ....
4. ....
5. ....
6. ....
7. ....
8. ....
9. ....
10. ....

I Feel
Write how your wins make you feel.

1. ....
2. ....
3. ....

Areas to Improve
Write these as "I will" statements.

1. ....
2. ....
3. ....

Notes:

My Daily Wins
Write your wins, no matter how small!

Date ....

1. ....
2. ....
3. ....
4. ....
5. ....
6. ....
7. ....
8. ....
9. ....
10. ....

I Feel
Write how your wins make you feel.

1. ....
2. ....
3. ....

Areas to Improve
Write these as "I will" statements.

1. ....
2. ....
3. ....

Notes:

My Daily Wins
Write your wins, no matter how small!

Date ....

1. ....
2. ....
3. ....
4. ....
5. ....
6. ....
7. ....
8. ....
9. ....
10. ....

I Feel
Write how your wins make you feel.

1. ....
2. ....
3. ....

Areas to Improve
Write these as "I will" statements.

1. ....
2. ....
3. ....

Notes:

My Daily Wins
Write your wins, no matter how small!

Date ....

1. ....
2. ....
3. ....
4. ....
5. ....
6. ....
7. ....
8. ....
9. ....
10. ....

I Feel
Write how your wins make you feel.

1. ....
2. ....
3. ....

Areas to Improve
Write these as "I will" statements.

1. ....
2. ....
3. ....

Notes:

My Daily Wins
Write your wins, no matter how small!

Date ....

1. ....
2. ....
3. ....
4. ....
5. ....
6. ....
7. ....
8. ....
9. ....
10. ....

I Feel
Write how your wins make you feel.

1. ....
2. ....
3. ....

Areas to Improve
Write these as "I will" statements.

1. ....
2. ....
3. ....

Notes:

My Daily Wins
Write your wins, no matter how small!

Date ....

1. ....
2. ....
3. ....
4. ....
5. ....
6. ....
7. ....
8. ....
9. ....
10. ....

I Feel
Write how your wins make you feel.

1. ....
2. ....
3. ....

Areas to Improve
Write these as "I will" statements.

1. ....
2. ....
3. ....

Notes:

My Daily Wins
Write your wins, no matter how small!

Date ....

1. ....
2. ....
3. ....
4. ....
5. ....
6. ....
7. ....
8. ....
9. ....
10. ....

I Feel
Write how your wins make you feel.

1. ....
2. ....
3. ....

Areas to Improve
Write these as "I will" statements.

1. ....
2. ....
3. ....

Notes:

My Daily Wins

Date ....

Write your wins, no matter how small!

1. ....
2. ....
3. ....
4. ....
5. ....
6. ....
7. ....
8. ....
9. ....
10. ....

I Feel

Write how your wins make you feel.

1. ....
2. ....
3. ....

Areas to Improve

Write these as "I will" statements.

1. ....
2. ....
3. ....

Notes:

My Daily Wins
Write your wins, no matter how small!

Date ....

1. ....
2. ....
3. ....
4. ....
5. ....
6. ....
7. ....
8. ....
9. ....
10. ....

I Feel
Write how your wins make you feel.

1. ....
2. ....
3. ....

Areas to Improve
Write these as "I will" statements.

1. ....
2. ....
3. ....

Notes:

My Daily Wins

Write your wins, no matter how small!

Date ....

1. ....
2. ....
3. ....
4. ....
5. ....
6. ....
7. ....
8. ....
9. ....
10. ....

I Feel

Write how your wins make you feel.

1. ....
2. ....
3. ....

Areas to Improve

Write these as "I will" statements.

1. ....
2. ....
3. ....

Notes:

My Daily Wins
Write your wins, no matter how small!

Date ....

1. ....
2. ....
3. ....
4. ....
5. ....
6. ....
7. ....
8. ....
9. ....
10. ....

I Feel
Write how your wins make you feel.

1. ....
2. ....
3. ....

Areas to Improve
Write these as "I will" statements.

1. ....
2. ....
3. ....

Notes:

My Daily Wins
Write your wins, no matter how small!

Date ....

1. ....
2. ....
3. ....
4. ....
5. ....
6. ....
7. ....
8. ....
9. ....
10. ....

I Feel
Write how your wins make you feel.

1. ....
2. ....
3. ....

Areas to Improve
Write these as "I will" statements.

1. ....
2. ....
3. ....

Notes:

My Daily Wins
Write your wins, no matter how small!

Date ....

1. ....
2. ....
3. ....
4. ....
5. ....
6. ....
7. ....
8. ....
9. ....
10. ....

I Feel
Write how your wins make you feel.

1. ....
2. ....
3. ....

Areas to Improve
Write these as "I will" statements.

1. ....
2. ....
3. ....

Notes:

My Daily Wins
Write your wins, no matter how small!

Date ....

1. ....
2. ....
3. ....
4. ....
5. ....
6. ....
7. ....
8. ....
9. ....
10. ....

I Feel
Write how your wins make you feel.

1. ....
2. ....
3. ....

Areas to Improve
Write these as "I will" statements.

1. ....
2. ....
3. ....

Notes:

My Daily Wins
Write your wins, no matter how small!

Date ....

1. ....
2. ....
3. ....
4. ....
5. ....
6. ....
7. ....
8. ....
9. ....
10. ....

I Feel
Write how your wins make you feel.

1. ....
2. ....
3. ....

Areas to Improve
Write these as "I will" statements.

1. ....
2. ....
3. ....

Notes:

My Daily Wins
Write your wins, no matter how small!

Date ....

1. ....
2. ....
3. ....
4. ....
5. ....
6. ....
7. ....
8. ....
9. ....
10. ....

I Feel
Write how your wins make you feel.

1. ....
2. ....
3. ....

Areas to Improve
Write these as "I will" statements.

1. ....
2. ....
3. ....

Notes:

My Daily Wins
Write your wins, no matter how small!

Date ....

1. ....
2. ....
3. ....
4. ....
5. ....
6. ....
7. ....
8. ....
9. ....
10. ....

I Feel
Write how your wins make you feel.

1. ....
2. ....
3. ....

Areas to Improve
Write these as "I will" statements.

1. ....
2. ....
3. ....

Notes:

My Daily Wins
Write your wins, no matter how small!

Date ....

1. ....
2. ....
3. ....
4. ....
5. ....
6. ....
7. ....
8. ....
9. ....
10. ....

I Feel
Write how your wins make you feel.

1. ....
2. ....
3. ....

Areas to Improve
Write these as "I will" statements.

1. ....
2. ....
3. ....

Notes:

My Daily Wins
Write your wins, no matter how small!

Date ....

1. ....
2. ....
3. ....
4. ....
5. ....
6. ....
7. ....
8. ....
9. ....
10. ....

I Feel
Write how your wins make you feel.

1. ....
2. ....
3. ....

Areas to Improve
Write these as "I will" statements.

1. ....
2. ....
3. ....

Notes:

My Daily Wins
Write your wins, no matter how small!

Date ....

1. ....
2. ....
3. ....
4. ....
5. ....
6. ....
7. ....
8. ....
9. ....
10. ....

I Feel
Write how your wins make you feel.

1. ....
2. ....
3. ....

Areas to Improve
Write these as "I will" statements.

1. ....
2. ....
3. ....

Notes:

My Daily Wins
Write your wins, no matter how small!

Date ....

1. ....
2. ....
3. ....
4. ....
5. ....
6. ....
7. ....
8. ....
9. ....
10. ....

I Feel
Write how your wins make you feel.

1. ....
2. ....
3. ....

Areas to Improve
Write these as "I will" statements.

1. ....
2. ....
3. ....

Notes:

My Daily Wins
Write your wins, no matter how small!

Date ....

1. ....
2. ....
3. ....
4. ....
5. ....
6. ....
7. ....
8. ....
9. ....
10. ....

I Feel
Write how your wins make you feel.

1. ....
2. ....
3. ....

Areas to Improve
Write these as "I will" statements.

1. ....
2. ....
3. ....

Notes:

My Daily Wins
Write your wins, no matter how small!

Date ....

1. ....
2. ....
3. ....
4. ....
5. ....
6. ....
7. ....
8. ....
9. ....
10. ....

I Feel
Write how your wins make you feel.

1. ....
2. ....
3. ....

Areas to Improve
Write these as "I will" statements.

1. ....
2. ....
3. ....

Notes:

My Daily Wins
Write your wins, no matter how small!

Date ....

1. ....
2. ....
3. ....
4. ....
5. ....
6. ....
7. ....
8. ....
9. ....
10. ....

I Feel
Write how your wins make you feel.

1. ....
2. ....
3. ....

Areas to Improve
Write these as "I will" statements.

1. ....
2. ....
3. ....

Notes:

My Daily Wins
Write your wins, no matter how small!

Date ....

1. ....
2. ....
3. ....
4. ....
5. ....
6. ....
7. ....
8. ....
9. ....
10. ....

I Feel
Write how your wins make you feel.

1. ....
2. ....
3. ....

Areas to Improve
Write these as "I will" statements.

1. ....
2. ....
3. ....

Notes:

My Daily Wins
Write your wins, no matter how small!

Date ....

1. ....
2. ....
3. ....
4. ....
5. ....
6. ....
7. ....
8. ....
9. ....
10. ....

I Feel
Write how your wins make you feel.

1. ....
2. ....
3. ....

Areas to Improve
Write these as "I will" statements.

1. ....
2. ....
3. ....

Notes:

My Daily Wins
Write your wins, no matter how small!

Date ....

1. ....
2. ....
3. ....
4. ....
5. ....
6. ....
7. ....
8. ....
9. ....
10. ....

I Feel
Write how your wins make you feel.

1. ....
2. ....
3. ....

Areas to Improve
Write these as "I will" statements.

1. ....
2. ....
3. ....

Notes:

Quarterly Wins

My Top Three Wins for the Last Quarter   Date ....
Write and reflect on the past quarter.

1. ....
2. ....
3. ....

My Wins Make Me Feel
Share how the wins from the last quarter make you feel.

1. ....
2. ....
3. ....

Areas Needing More Time and Work
Write these as "I will" statements.

1. ....
2. ....
3. ....

Notes:

Notes

Notes

Notes

Notes

Notes

Notes

Notes

Notes

Notes

Notes

Printed in the USA
CPSIA information can be obtained
at www.ICGtesting.com
LVHW071913170823
755550LV00015B/199